I CUT MY FINGER

Other books by Stuart Ross

Confessions of a Small Press Racketeer (Anvil Press, 2005)
Robots at Night (Proper Tales Press, 2005)
Hey, Crumbling Balcony! Poems New & Selected (ECW Press, 2003)
Me & the Pope (Proper Tales Press, 2002)
Razovsky at Peace (ECW Press, 2001)
Home Shopping (Room 302 Books, 2000)
Farmer Gloomy's New Hybrid (ECW Press, 1999)
The Results of the Autopsy: 13 Little Love Stories (Proper Tales Press, 1999)
Mr. Joe (Proper Tales Press, 1998)
Language Lessons with Simon and Marie! (as Estuardo Rossini; Proper Tales Press, 1998)
Henry Kafka & Other Stories (The Mercury Press, 1997)
Poemas 4 Cuentos 1 (Proper Tales Press, 1996)
The Inspiration Cha-Cha (ECW Press, 1996)
The Mud Game (w/ Gary Barwin, The Mercury Press, 1995)
Dusty Hats Vanish (Proper Tales Press, 1994)
Kruger (Proper Tales Press, 1994)
The Pig Sleeps (w/ Mark Laba, Contra Mundo Books, 1993)
Runts (Proper Tales Press Press, 1992)
In This World (Silver Birch Press, 1992)
Mister Style, That's Me (Proper Tales Press, 1991)
Guided Missiles (Proper Tales Press, 1990)
Smothered (Contra Mundo Press, 1990)
Ladies & Gentlemen, Mr. Ron Padgett (Proper Tales Press, 1989)
Bunnybaby: The Child with Magnificent Ears (Proper Tales Press, 1988)
Paralysis Beach (Pink Dog Press, 1988)
Captain Earmuff's Agenda (The Front Press, 1987)
Wooden Rooster (Proper Tales Press, 1986)
Skip & Biff Cling to the Radio (Proper Tales Press, 1984)
Father, the Cowboys Are Ready to Come Down from the Attic (Proper Tales Press, 1982)
When Electrical Sockets Walked Like Men (Proper Tales Press, 1981)
Bad Glamour (Proper Tales Press, 1980)
He Counted His Fingers, He Counted His Toes (Proper Tales Press, 1979)

ANTHOLOGIES:

Surreal Estate: 13 Canadian Writers Under the Influence (The Mercury Press, 2004)
My Lump in the Bed: Love Poems for George W. Bush (Proper Tales Press, 2004)
Time to Kill Boss (Proper Tales Press, 2002)
Primitive Bubble And (Proper Tales Press, 2001)

I CUT MY FINGER

Stuart Ross

ANVIL PRESS | 2007

Copyright © 2007 by Stuart Ross

Anvil Press Inc.
P.O. Box 3008, Main Post Office
Vancouver, B.C. V6B 3X5 canada
www.anvilpress.com

All rights reserved. No part of this book may be reproduced by any means without the prior written permission of the publisher, with the exception of brief passages in reviews. Any request for photocopying or other reprographic copying of any part of this book must be directed in writing to access: The Canadian Copyright Licensing Agency, One Yonge Street, Suite 800, Toronto, Ontario, Canada, M5E 1E5.

LIBRARY AND ARCHIVES CANADA CATALOGUING IN PUBLICATION

Ross, Stuart

    I cut my finger / Stuart Ross.

Poems.

ISBN 978-1-895636-79-6

    I. Title.

PS8585.O841I17 2007   C811'.54   C2007-901759-2

Printed and bound in Canada
Cover illustration and design: Gary Clement
Interior design & typesetting: HeimatHouse

Represented in Canada by the Literary Press Group
Distributed by the University of Toronto Press

The publisher gratefully acknowledges the financial assistance of the Canada Council for the Arts, the Book Publishing Industry Development Program (BPIDP), and the Province of British Columbia through the B.C. Arts Council and the Book Publishing Tax Credit.

Table of Contents

The Door	9
I Cut My Finger	10
A Thrush	12
The Church Has a Church Beside It	13
The Surface	14
A Guy, Some Flippers, a Building	16
Song	17
How I Became Exquisite	18
An Orphan	20
The Ocean	21
The Coup	22
November: Launch	24
Monday Morning, August	25
Razovsky in Space	26
Civilization Sonnet	28
Self-Portrait	29
Work	30
Haiku	32
They Gathered Before the Circus Arrived	33
Others Like Me	34
A Traumatic High School Tap-Dancing Incident	35
Sediment	36
Assassin	37
The Bed	39
Song	40

I Left My Heart In	41
The Effect of Rock	43
Frisky	44
This Slow Dazzle	45
Me and Soupy	46
The Mountain	47
Beginning	48
After Carrots	49
Mary Is the Merry One	50
Fishing	52
New Hope for the Disenfranchised	53
What's Important Now	55
Always Happen in a Dusk	57
Poem	58
The Blizzard	59
Experiments in Oral Suction and Gill Breathing in Five Species of Australian Tadpole	60
Wealth Kingdom	61
The Virus Cabin	62
Poem	63
Robots at Night	64
Razovsky by Numbers	65
I Open the Lid	67
One Fine Afternoon in New Denver, B.C.	68
2 Kootenay Poems	71
Submission	72
Fragment	75

Song	76
Capitalism	77
The Boy Who Waited Three Minutes	79
I Step Off the Plane	81
Across the Border	83
A True History of the Netherlands	85
In a Village Just Off Exit 47	87
Because One Thing Bumped into Another	88
TV Listings	89
My Lapel	90
Ermine and Pearls	92
"I Speak English, Wall Street English"	94
Adjustment	95
50 O'clock	96
Bathurst and St. Clair, 11:43 P.M.	97
Sonnet for the New Year	98
Letter for Saturday (January 1, 2005)	99
Poem for Sunday (January 1, 2006)	100
Razovsky and the River of Blindness	101
Notes	103
About the Author	104

THE DOOR

I approach the door.
The door approaches the Welcome mat.
The Welcome mat approaches the stairs.
The stairs approach the flagstone path.
The flagstone path approaches the curb.
The curb approaches the street.
The street approaches
the topic gingerly,
cowering behind the bushes
that hide the naked dog.

I CUT MY FINGER

A mountain was on the ground.
I don't know how it got there, probably a thing
regarding the earth.
I walked up it quick but it was high
and took a long time. I thought
maybe Mom and Dad and Owen would be there,
or at least floating above it.
Oh the adventures I had climbing,
let me recount them (in case I counted
wrong the first time). Numerous
calendar pages flipped by
like in a movie you saw,
and then I was on top.

I tried calling Dana but there wasn't any phone
and I cut my finger
dialing a rock. The bad thing was
there was nobody up there,
and nobody floating above.
Not even a store when I felt like Chiclets.

But I could feel my tired brain wobbling,
and I sat down and got ready to think:
and then I thought: I thought that for me
mountains are big solid things poking into the air,
like at god,
but for people for whom solid
is the absence of solid,

then they've got upside-down mountains
pointing towards earth.

I rested a bit,
then came back down.

A THRUSH

A thrush darted through their field
of vision, and they changed
the channel, just like that,
to where hundreds of people
stood at the edge of a desert canyon,
peering down at a smouldering disco.
On another channel, something calamitous
took place in my living room
and I looked all around me
but couldn't see any cameras
nor any calamity. I pulled back
my lips and ran a fingernail
between two teeth, and there
it was, that thing that had been
bugging me: it was a horseshoe.
I too once was nailed to the foot
of a horse, we call these *hooves*,
and a thrush flit by my window
and I counted the days till tomorrow.

THE CHURCH HAS A CHURCH BESIDE IT

for Gunnar Kopperud

Jungle comrade,
drive me to the cows,
the sheep,
into the hills
— far from the wretched kebaberies of Oslo
and the fierce bronze poodle of Olaf
that rustles with threat
in the brief night.
Bring me up to the cemetery
by the side of the narrow road,
where there is a church and
also a church beside it.
Tell me the saga of the surgeon
who separated the conjoined churches,
of the priest who loved
two sisters, or the choir
so magnificent they built
another church for the overflow.
Jungle comrade,
leave me on the banks
of the murmuring fjord.
Introduce me
to your friends in the ice.

THE SURFACE

The words agonized over their own inertia.
I took back my woolen gloves,
grieving for my lovers, my desk drawers,
my occasional waves of dusk.
A conversation:
the long night flung meaning
into the stars. I clutched
my covers to my neck.
I had become holy, but also
I had become a monster.
Terrible things drifted above my roof,
whose shingles kiss the breeze. A spell.
A skull. It is my birthday.
It is sleep. Our together is the surface
of our innocence, or ourselves.
I extinguish my mouth, my future.
Inspiration comes. An auction of promise
lays its long pale legs beside me.
But I repeat myself. In the distance:
a description of love. You came to me,
I came to me, the schoolhouse came to me,
the formal sorrow.
                    In darkness,
the first act unfolded. We dreamt
of the woman in the box office.
She slept urgently amid the words.
At any rate,
we had become primitive,

*consumer products offering
decreased services, denying
ourselves sleep.
            I recognized
my eyelids. I could pick them out
in a lineup. They
renounced me. A bird flew close
and then shot out into
the sponginess of the slinking stars.*

A GUY, SOME FLIPPERS, A BUILDING

He got his flippers on
and it made him go swimming.
It was tough, but he kept on swimming.
Then he saw the water was pavement
and he remembered his grandpa's words:
"Pavement is the hard one.
You don't need your flippers for it."
He racked his brains to recall
what "don't" meant and meanwhile
he bumped his head on a building.
A building's a square thing with a hole inside
where people live or maybe work.
Inside the building that bumped his head,
a woman made copies of a sheet of paper
with writing on it, and while she made copies,
she thought about a river
and the way she could float on her back
on top of it, on the part where it met the air.
Above, the sky was crammed with clouds.
A bird was a dark thing in it.

SONG

In the night
a gunshot
is in the night.
The bullet ricochets
off the Andes
and enters the brain
of a leaping brown rabbit.

The dogs, which had been barking all night, go silent.

Then they go crazy.
The dogs go crazy
under the dark sky
that fills up the space
above my roof.
In the vineyard,
a man holds a pistol.
As he spreads out his arms,
a song rises from his chest.

HOW I BECAME EXQUISITE

There in my favourite bar, Legends,
whose walls were plastered
with photos of Theodor Herzl
and that girl who sang
"You Light Up My Life,"
plus also an unshaven Fred Flintstone
shaking hands with Pierre Trudeau
and smirking into the camera,
I was about to order
the chicken curry with basmati rice
and a big glass of milk
when I noticed Misery
hanging by the jukebox.
A draft nearly knocked me over
as Thelma the waitress came in from her smoke,
and I pulled my coat tighter,
and she pulled hers looser,
and I found myself at the jukebox.
"Would you like a little company?" I said,
and just as he parted his lips to answer,
I let Misery have one
right in the stomach. (Not
the actual organ itself,
but the place on his body
where the stomach is under.)
He crumpled and fell
to the peanut-shell-strewn floor, and I,
having punched out Misery,

divested myself of my mortal clothes
and draped me in a robe of magenta.
I assumed a new way of walking
that signalled my importance,
I mean, I got really robust,
and glided through the streets,
my head on an ivory-encrusted tray,
approaching stray orphans
and offering them some.

AN ORPHAN

An orphan stands on a balcony singing something that would become popular in the next century. His papa takes notice, and licks him with a tongue of flame. An office building blows by, hugged in the arms of a schoolgirl. The roiling clouds assume the shape of a giant eyeball and gaze down approvingly.

A spider hides in an ashtray, trembling amid the cigarette butts. An orphan lies on the sofa, coughing and sweating, clutching the channel-changer. In the kitchen, a miracle occurs in the fridge, then goes back to normal. First the curtains are sucked out the window, then everything else.

Aroused after crawling such a long way, a mirror french-kisses a dirty puddle. The sign above the billiards hall begins to sneeze, from all the chalk. An orphan sees his mama in the eye of a baked potato, the eye of a baked potato. A cry breaks free from a plastic bag.

A production of *The Mikado* is cancelled because none of its cast is human. The legs of a bed are peppered with mosquito bites. An act of desperation flosses its teeth, trying to look its best for church. An orphan buries an abacus on a beach beside an empty ocean.

THE OCEAN

The government was bugging me.
I was gloomy.
CNN was on in the background.
A thing about guys getting killed
because other guys were mean.
I was playing chess
with a guy who lived near the ocean.
I did this with my computer.
I told him the ocean's
got a lot of water in it,
it's full of fish.
After he checkmated me,
he walked out his door.
The ocean *was* full of water!
He waded in
and saw there were fish.
He ate them with French fries.
Later in the day,
he sliced up a lemon,
put it in a pitcher of water.
He refreshed all his friends.
When he slept that night,
the ocean peered through his window.

THE COUP

The retired generals are turning.
Once they got people
to kill people but now
they notice fine white strands
spiraling from the edges of
certain kinds of leaves.
They follow trails of red ants
and go, "Look at all the red ants!
Those sure are a lot of red ants!"
They take a road trip and
really like the playground
at the Davidson Motel
in Paris, Ontario, and fight
over the teeter-totter,
but only play-fight. There's time
for everyone to have a turn.

The Secretary of Defense, meanwhile,
his lip is quivering. His right toe
pokes out his sock. He doesn't like it
when people say bad things
about him. He has no patience
for insubordination. He goes to
the dictionary to look up
"insubordination" but the words
all look like random scribblings.
They look like the sound
ducks make. Even worse.

Out the window, a glacier slides by.
All these things
happen on it.

NOVEMBER: LAUNCH

at dark
the highway

between Paris
and Toronto

shimmers

pointing
every direction

Nelson and Barbara
stay home
sit in the kitchen

launching
grey cups
of black coffee
to their pale lips

silent
content

MONDAY MORNING, AUGUST

The paper-thin grey
membrane of the bat's wing
slap slap slaps
against the priest's
wide and glistening
forehead. Beneath
his feet, the pebbles crunch
like peppercorns. A
cluster of children,
their books
slung over their shoulders,
sneeze. A butterfly
is carried into the sun
by the morning breeze.
I sit on the curb
counting my slender
white fingers. Look!
Five to a hand!
Last time I counted,
there were only four.

RAZOVSKY IN SPACE

The aisles are cramped,
the hardwood floor covered
in sawdust and raisins. Razovsky
takes slow and unsteady steps,
fingertips grazing the shelves
that rise taller than his grey hair
on either side. It smells
of mothballs here, but also
hot chocolate, and from the back room
the sound of a sewing machine:
the rise and fall of a cast-iron pedal,
the staccato insistence of hems
being stitched.
                 A minute ago,
Razovsky'd been floating in space,
false teeth drifting by, and hunks
of metal, flashing like cameras.
In a photo album somewhere
back on earth, Razovsky stands grinning
in a field just off a single-lane road,
his black hair flickering
in a barely perceptible breeze.
His long coat, too, is black, and his arm
wraps around a woman in fur
who laughs at the camera. Behind them,
the sky is clear, blends into the photo's
border, and a thin band of leafless trees
reaches across the horizon.

                        When he gets to
the back of the shop, Razovsky pushes aside
a curtain, steps into a tiny room
lit by a single light bulb. A man in a vest
and rolled-up white sleeves
turns from his Singer sewing machine.
It is Blatt. A few strands of white hair
lie on his glistening scalp, and a strand
of black thread hangs
from the corner of his mouth. Blatt
was an astronaut, too, once. He points
to a chair and Razovsky sits down.
They strap themselves in
and wait for lift-off.

CIVILIZATION SONNET

Out of the flabby sky, water began to leak.
In the synagogue, the gritty plumber slept.
Wet became the new dry. Celebrate.
There was only one bag of Fritos
to share among us, and they said eternity
was longer than a week.
I try to eat good,
like lettuce, but
you get hands and they get
dirty. Let's get organized.
I'm after the lady
with the monkey in her carriage.
I was before, but
I let her go first.

SELF-PORTRAIT

He saw his image.
A dense day stuck
to his arrival. He swam
out of his own eyes.
He intercepted a stupid pope,
restless, raining, in pain.
A movement poses for its portrait,
a tender, restrained secret
spurting from its soul.
He sought a mirror,
struck a posture of evening,
placed his hand flat
against his large forehead,
a wall that separates his words
from his tongue.
Anything embraces a dull balloon,
its teeth in yesterday's fragments.
A silent dream filtered
his on-and-on, irregular remains.
The breathless seasons fly off
the wheels of trucks, revealing
firm acceptance. The strewn distance
completed its artful chores.

WORK

A collection of skulls
was not unusual among
those we interviewed. Swans
circled their backyard
swimming pools, where
murky figures rippled
at the bottom. My knees
hurt as I climbed a long
staircase to the Room
That Holds The Ledgers,
and I thought of my wife,
Pascha, seventeen years dead,
who had greeted me each
morning with a cheerful
"God has you by the throat
for another day," and I'd
make her breakfast, kiss
our imaginary children.
I did what I had to
to make ends meet:
I'd been a sailor, a
painter of artificial
eyeballs, and the guy
on whom they try
those little hammers
the doctors use to
make you kick your
legs.

Where was I?
Right, the top of the stairs
where there awaited a
particular kind of splendour,
an eccentric panache,
a game of Am I Grinning
Or Am I Grimacing
that I'd long since tired of.
It pays the rent, but
who among us — us
being those who must
climb the stairs in spite of bad knees
— does not yearn
to turn our back on
all these numerals, these
cups of cold tea, the
servants, the servants,
the marble toilets,
the crustless slices
of marbled bread,
and Roger and Tootsie
Saliva-Whitechapel, and
spend the days that remain
bound in a corset,
gasping for breath,
laughing at those movies
they used to make,
the ones with no words.

HAIKU

There are bugs
in the wilderness —
with antennae!

THEY GATHERED BEFORE
THE CIRCUS ARRIVED

Bumpy was wearing the stupidest hat at the picnic,
But no one commented due to his ailment.
They hoisted ales and looked far into the sky
From whence plopped down their ancestors
How long a time ago I do not remember.

Who could help but exhale on so peaceful a day,
So far from the hacking lead pipes that ran from the toilet
To the glistening, sticky depths of Lake Ontario?
They drank to that, and drank to it again, as spores danced by.

A goat wandered sheepishly from under the steeple,
Its buttocks a-rattle with lottery tickets and castanets.
The fantastic blue circus would soon arrive
And they would lay Bumpy in a pile of hay,
At the foot of the elephant, beneath the trapeze.

OTHERS LIKE ME

Sun filled my eyes
and grass warmed my feet.
I pressed my fists
into my chest
to confirm
that I was alive.
Certain things
suggested I was:
for example, the fact
of no answer, no end,
no gas station attendant.
Others like me appeared,
coughing, snickering, crying.
We fought, fucked,
built a society,
and set out
to construct
a sailboat from toothpicks,
books from the wings
of an aphid.

A TRAUMATIC HIGH SCHOOL
TAP-DANCING INCIDENT

The detectives found an unusual
substance on the walls and sniffed
each other's shoes and ears. The principal
clutched his debating trophy
from 1972 and shivered. The janitor,
who once turned tricks
in a bowling alley, incinerated
everything and invited us
to watch it burn. A window slammed shut
on the second floor
and broke Sheldon Teicher's fingers.
His chemistry teacher screamed. A beaker
fell to the floor and exploded.

But here's what I wanted to tell you:
Miriam Cohen and Hedy Cohen,
who were not sisters, not even
related, were practising
for the talent assembly,
their taps in sublime synchronicity,
when Mr. Cohen, who was
one of them's father,
shouted through the window
from out in the parking lot:
something about
a baloney sandwich
with mustard.

SEDIMENT

Like when Murray Nightingale
brought a cow's heart to school
in a big pickle jar. His dad
owned a slaughterhouse and Murray
was always bringing parts of cows
to school. The heart was white
and the jar afloat with sediment.
In Murray's speech about the invasion
of Czechoslovakia, he said that as
the tanks rolled through the streets,
the Czechs lined the curbs
with "grims" on their faces. Or
was that Clifford Snider,
or Cy Stanway, or little Gary Weinberg?
A few years later, Mr. Joshua had us
spit into test tubes. I asked him
about the sediment on the bottom.
"That's mucus," said Mr. Joshua.
Today I find I have fewer friends
every ten minutes. They flee
my hideous crimes and what they leave behind
is that a better poet than me
would insert a really good sediment
metaphor right here. (Or, more poignantly,
here.)

ASSASSIN

Constantinople, after the big storm:
a spit of flame, a thud.
A man stretched out on a marble floor.
It's like he's sleeping. *Remember:
When the sun shines, it shines
for all, not just the rich.*
Another man drops a pistol into a sewer,
skidding across the plaza on his heels.
He falls into a casual stride, but
his head is about to explode,
he feels eyes
boring into his flesh. Several years
later, and then a year after that,
he is reading a daily on a terrace.
He doesn't follow a word.
He can't stop knowing
what he has done. Silently
he prays, the Sports page
rattling in his fingers. In
Jerusalem, he shivers at night,
presses fingertips to temples.
*There's room for everyone.
Literally: there is air for every nostril.*
Are the sounds he hears
the sounds that everyone hears?
Everything closes around him. In day-
light he hurtles through the clay streets
muttering French rhymes from his

childhood. The phone rings
in his empty hotel room, the curtains
fluttering. Flies crawl upon
his unmade bed.

THE BED

The rectangle of the bed was shoved into the corner of the rectangle of the room. He lay in them, in both the room and the bed. He was narrower but longer than the bed and spilled over it accordingly. But when he became diagonal, he fit. He favoured this — diagonality. Over his head, he heard an airplane fly slowly past. Between him and the airplane was a ceiling. It sealed off his view of the airplane. And so he had only his room to look at. A lighting fixture on the ceiling contained several dead flies, but only when it was on. He thought about electrocution. And he thought about hats with ear flaps. It was such a long walk to school, he knew he'd arrive the next day. He tried to feel the sky against his face, and heard his mother laugh in another room. But when they went to bury her, their spades rang out: the ground was frozen.

SONG

They live in the mud, those
who we've placed there,
and those who were slammed there
by sudden waters.

I crouch in the snow
at my mother's feet
and count the stones
placed on her head.

There to my left
lies my father, always quiet,
and a couple rows over
my brother, a baseball cap on his chest.

They are joined, those
who live in the mud,
and we too are joined
who wail on the snow and wail on the beach.

1 January 2005

I LEFT MY HEART IN

I go to bed one dark night
thinking I'm catching a cold,
there's a distant tickle in my throat,
and when I awake I am
Siamese twins. Some say now
I enjoy things twice as much
and some say only half as much,
but I cup my hand to my right profile
and try to pretend that nothing has changed.

And nothing *has* changed!
The wind sweeps snow along the black streets
and invisible sparrows call from the branches.
Billowing clouds somersault through the sky
assuming the shapes of dead prime ministers.
Sausages burst from sausage machines,
and the horse pulling the milk cart stumbles.
I have an education in my head
and one in each hand, I can build
anything, I can build anything!
and the boy beside me
who I've never seen, though we share flesh
and an organ or two,
he writes an autobiography
without ever mentioning me.

There is a tomorrow in which
I drift into the sky, and the earth

becomes a wee dot, so tiny
it disappears, and you are on it
so you vanish too. But you only
vanish to me — to you, you are
still here and you clutch your violin
or perhaps it's your baby,
it's hard to tell, and the boy
beside you holds a violin too.
I wish I'd had a brother like that.

THE EFFECT OF ROCK

One night when something else is happening,
a big rock flies close to Earth
but nobody notices
(because of the other thing).
It has bugs on it.
The sky remains blue
and there is no discernable effect
on wind velocity or
the grittiness of egrets.
People's heads, though,
begin to get real big
until they have to walk around
with head braces radiating from their hips.
Now hats are useless.
Now yarmulkas are too little.
Now burkhas burst open and women are stoned.
Sweaters don't fit over people's heads
and headphones can't reach.
The Red Cross widens people's doorways
so their heads don't get wedged going through.
They use sledgehammers.
Other things result that I can't think of now.
But, meanwhile, the rock with the bugs
keeps flying through space.
When it passes a planet with heads on it,
the heads get bigger, a trail of bigger heads.
The bugs don't know what havoc they've spread.
They're just bugs.
Life is hard for them.

FRISKY

Ron Padgett
flexed his body
in mid-air, turned
and yelped

It was his birthday
and he was sixty-two

THIS SLOW DAZZLE

for Dana Samuel

This brilliant image
in a tiny square
of video screen
hovers before
my beet-red face.
This calming warmth.
This tender question
raked through my wiry hair.
This precise outrage
of ingenious surprises.
You walk forward,
sonic beauty
cutting an auction of flames.
Onstage he puts
his perfect viola
to his chin,
and I cram catastrophe
into the farthest corner.
Affection is a street
named after you.
I dream I am a breeze
through your window.

ME AND SOUPY

I was waiting for a bus at
the corner of Beeswax
and Latrine, and
a child who looked exactly
like me as a child
walked by. My
jaw dropped, and he
heard the clank and
picked it up off the sidewalk,
and as he handed my jaw to me,
he said, "You're Soupy Sales!"

At the mouth of the river there's a bent-up old lawn chair
into which each morning I heave my spent carcass
and there I heaved myself, or hefted myself,
and I thought of the child
that was me before I was Soupy Sales,
and I pressed my face into the prayer book
and smelled the old people around me, and in me,
as coloured light fell on the backs of my hands,
and Moses was a puppet, and King David a puppet,
and a withered old hand of a beautiful woman
stroked my bent shoulder through my tallit.

THE MOUNTAIN

I stood on the peak of the mountain, or perhaps only halfway up, I hardly remember now, it was so long ago. Or perhaps just last week — who can keep such details straight? I mean, I've barely put fork to mouth and food to brain, though I sit in front of the TV with my Roy Rogers dinner tray, watching the sitcom of my tragic life, punctuated by waltzing couples with painted-on hair and commercials for kilometre-long strands of cheese. If I close my eyes tight, the stars that are spread across the black sky cluster instantly, like thousands of tiny spiders on a web sparkling damply at the first hint of sun peeking into the vineyards. I can reach out and close my fist around them, push them into my mouth, or into my pants pocket, or maybe the shoebox I keep under my bed. Look: when I leap straight up, sometimes I plummet immediately, splaying onto the pavement like a puppet, but sometimes I stay up in the air for a few minutes, and those are minutes I treasure: weightless, I contort my limbs into artful designs or Hebrew characters, or simply let the streams of air do with me what they will. As the sun sinks into the saddle, I jam my toe into what looks like solid dirt, but it's nothing but dust and dung and dried twigs, and I skid and flail towards the abyss. The effect is so comical, I'm offered a contract as a cartoon character.

BEGINNING

I walked for so long, I followed
the steps of pointy ladders.
A century of privilege
scudded down a flooded slope,
until they gathered for the war:
the banjo, the fiddle,
and the cheese sandwich.
At 4 o'clock,
solitude knocked on my door. My frock
is stained, human. The fatigued
executives are frightened.
We have waited for the expiration
of the soup's quiet.
Time is funny, like a shaft of primrose.
We are doomed. We begin.
We are doomed. We begin.
A cactus passes by.
I wake up, pure and persnickety,
and I rain, chasing my own drops.
Children, like ripening plums,
pack me away, attach their boats to me.
Them is bedazzled, whole,
a balcony of sobbing movement.

AFTER CARROTS

After carrots,
asparagus. After
that, a leap
into the roiling
cauldron of lunch.
I can't
explain to you
how I
arrived here, or
where next,
dogs snapping
at my ankles.
I pour
concrete into abstraction
and place
my fingertips
on your eyelids.
I remember
how close
the ground once
looked, but now
it's further away
each day.
The sun
cups us in
its cool palm
and feeds us
pieces
of what
we remember.

MARY IS THE MERRY ONE

Do you go to many parties?
We joined a party of hunters.
It pays to be particular in choosing a friend.
Sally is my particular friend.

The frog leaped into the pond.
The soldier has a four-day leave.
Professor Smythe is a learned man.
Who is the leader of this group?

The present is an age of jet travel.
How many presents did you get?
We preserved some science specimens in alcohol.
What a preposterous story!

The troops will gather, then attack.
The students gathered the books.
There are many kinds of games.
The hockey player has a game leg.

May we buy a miniature poodle?
The rescue was a miracle.
Mary is the merry one, but Sally is the merriest of all.
A mighty shove released the stone.

Frankenstein wore a hideous mask.
The robbery was a hoax.
No girl wishes to be homely.
A hobo does not work.

A wet puppy is a pitiful sight.
It's fun to play in a pile of leaves.
Who is the pitcher for the senior team?
Where is the milk pitcher?

Rotten vegetables emit offensive odours.
What an odd way to build a house!
Old people like company.
Offer him some money.

The rough actions of some people are unnecessary.
His singing roused the whole family.
Dinner was served in a royal manner.
The nurse rubbed my sore arm.

The science talk was about amphibians.
Kate has a talent for drawing.
The swollen river overflowed its banks.
That's a swell idea!

Astronauts have adventures in space.
Father advised me to stay in school.
The whole sky was aglow at sunset.
Opening night will be a splendid affair.

FISHING

    Oh right, that time
    he caught a fish, a fish
    so big it ate his car,
    his family, his
    cottage. A thing of
    sleek beauty, it gleamed
    and twinkled in the
    police spotlight. The
    bullet it caught
    lodged behind its left
    gill, and Jesus
    wept, the fish
    wept, we all fell
    to the ground
    and wept, sweet fish.

NEW HOPE FOR THE DISENFRANCHISED

It was at that exact moment, when
I began to empty my pockets,
which were empty to begin with,
except for a bent paperclip
and a tennis court oeuf (an
athletic and popular omelette,
sprinkled with pocket lint),
that my children returned from the future,
from long after my sorry death,
where they were quite comfortable and,
I was happy to hear,
saw each other often and spoke of me
not unkindly, if infrequently.
"I was just emptying my pockets,"
I told them, "liberating myself
from all things material, but look,
let's go to the zoo!" "The zoo!" they cried.
As we ambled amongst the apes,
my eldest, whose name I no longer
remember, gone from my noggin
along with my own, said to me,
"Everything's different later on.
A guy got shot
and hubbub ensued,
but when the dust settled, Dad,
it was a whole other thing."
Flanked by lemurs and ostriches,
I gathered my children

within the arc
of my fatherly arms.
I knew now that after I croaked,
a guy would get shot
and all would be better.
With the penguins looking on,
and under the gaze of giant turtles,
I kissed each of my children
(it took nearly an hour) upon
their foreheads, and I set off
for home. I had children
to conceive, a blender to fix,
rectangular books
to return to the library.

WHAT'S IMPORTANT NOW

A wall stops me!
I can get most of the front of me
against it. It feels good on me.
The wall is cool and ungiving.
I turn parts of me sideways,
like my head and my feet
and more of me gets
against the wall. I can hear
me breathing. My eyelids
clang shut like prison doors.
The downside is:
things go undone. Bills
accumulate, my children
lack a role model, the grass
gets real long. Also,
my hair. The president
drives a wedge between
those not against the wall
and those — me — who are.
I become cynical about
the democratic system.
The newspapers
call me "a long hair" but I think
they mean "a long-hair." The things
I did before the wall, these
seem like the doings
of another person.
What's important now

is more of me getting
against the wall. In this
I shall be resolute.

ALWAYS HAPPEN IN A DUSK

The sun goes away.
Shivering commences.
Cheap love in a house ensues.
A tree bends over from the wind.

Cancer is a baddy.
We got muscles in us now.
Parents look after the little ones.

A raccoon lights a cigarette.
Now I must rest on a pillow.

POEM

He ran around in tight circles.
He looked for a way out.
If there was no way out,
how did he get in?

Both out and in
were inside him.
How did they get there?

He stopped running.
He thought hard.
He stopped thinking.
He ran around in tight circles.

THE BLIZZARD

The car wants to be
like Fred or Ginger
but it is in crisis,
driven by a hermit crab,
skidding inexorably toward
a ditch, a snout-gouged
crevice, remembering its
pedal-car childhood, its
magnificent trip to Niagara Falls.
It feels awkward, like a
big slab of metal, its
glasses held on with tape
and snot on its upper
lip. The car feels its
flesh fold into itself,
its belly collapse, its
heart on fire. Eyes closed,
it lies in the ditch. Cars
dart by on the highway. Cars
choose to see what
they choose to see.

EXPERIMENTS IN ORAL SUCTION AND GILL BREATHING IN FIVE SPECIES OF AUSTRALIAN TADPOLE

I slept encased in the cement of the balcony.
A chimp lay nestled in each of my nostrils.
In the apartment above, a man read the last rites
to his TV set, and in the apartment below,
lusty raccoons screeched in the shower.

"Remember the days," she said, "when we met?
You wore a white smock
and plucked your grey eyebrows."
Far above her piled-up hair, two planets collided,
and civilizations were gone in an instant.

A head becomes full with too many regrets.
A bead of a chemical hangs from a dropper.

WEALTH KINGDOM

for Mark Truscott

When Marlon Perkins dies,
he belongs to everyone —
not just those
who cried
or he caught.

THE VIRUS CABIN

We holiday at the virus cabin.
At night, board games.
Vehicles pierce the walls.
A Mexican eye doctor blinks.
Soon we are bereft of cabbage.
The admiral collapses in a pool of sweat.
After the earthquake, we pack our things.
We lick abundant tears
from each other's cheeks.
Spring brings summer.
Summer brings grief.
The clouds, dark as coal,
draw the blankets over Baby's face.
"Keep talking," Bubbles whispers in my ear.
The microbes make us beautiful.
We climb upon one another and grunt.

POEM

> "I opened the window but don't remember
> Opening it, or someone else opened it"
> — Larry Fagin, "Poem"

Still,
two sandpipers
on my window sill,
their bills unpaid.
Cigarettes pack
the ashtray with themselves.
Art is on my walls,
which are arter than
my neighbour's walls.
I roll out of my bed,
onto the floor,
and under my bed.
There I await you,
clutching a bouquet
of forsythias
for Sythia.

ROBOTS AT NIGHT

Dear occupant: I think
you left one of your robots on.
Is there any way of turning it off
so it doesn't continue speaking
all night long? For relief,
I pushed open my window,
plunging my tired pale face
into the cold dark air of November,
and the rattle of streetcars
along the tracks and flashing lights
from the Happy Chow Mein
set the machinery of my brain
in motion, made me realize they
didn't hate me in junior high,
it was simply that they were all
so self-absorbed, and I was just
the daughter of the man who
invented Times Square
between runs to return the empties
and shootsies in the stairwell.

RAZOVSKY BY NUMBERS

The tumbling shelves
of button-filled jars, the dandelions
dotting the glistening lawn.
In the cupboard beneath the sink,
dented tins of shoe polish: black, brown,
red-brown. The rags that spilled
from the bottom drawer, from every
bottom drawer. And in the garage,
the nest of rusted pliers,
snapping, creaking.
Razovsky counted everything.

His fingers never stopped moving,
like his lips, and his eyeballs. He
inventoried, enumerated, catalogued,
whispered the names of all things,
and the things
that had no names. He counted dead uncles
he'd never met, each strand in their
long white beards, the threads
that hung from the cuffs of their
trousers. Razovsky counted
the sons they'd never had,
and the sons of the sons,
and he gave them all names.

"You're a Razovsky,
and you a Razovsky, and your

name's Razovsky, and I'll call you
Razovsky." And he counted each one
on a separate finger, because that
is what he did, he counted,
and when he ran out of fingers,
he used his toes, and then
the stones in his pockets, the teeth
in his mouth, the eyes on the fly
on the window ledge,
the scampering legs of a silverfish.

And when he was done,
he sat down with them, and
he counted the chairs around
the table, and counted the prayers
that had never been uttered,
and the prayers choked by smoke,
and Razovsky knew then who he was,
and he pinned a tag
to his shirt: "Razovsky."

I OPEN THE LID

after Joe Brainard

I open the lid. A butterfly. Its wings ragged and faded. Its legs scattered.

I open the lid. A dark stain. The tongue of a cow on a cutting board.

I open the lid. A page torn out from a spiral-bound notebook, the size I usually use. The paper is lined. In my own handwriting: "Close the box, you stupid fuck."

I open the lid. A ginger kitten looks up at me. Its eyes like ju-jubes.

I open the lid. A tangled mass of elastic bands. Some are red, some green, but most are elastic-band-coloured.

I open the lid. A broken clock.

I open the lid. A mirror in a plain pine frame. In it, my brother. My father stands behind him, cups his jaw, kisses the top of his head.

I open the lid. A black sock with thin white stripes. It stirs.

ONE FINE AFTERNOON IN NEW DENVER, B.C.

for Terry Taylor

At the top of the Salmo-Creston Pass,
amid the snow-capped peaks,
I stop my car and weep.
A guy from Nelson
in a levitating four-by-four
pulls over and hands me
a fortune cookie frosted with ice:
"Surrender yourself," it says,
"to the irresistible pull."

In the centre of Slocan Lake,
the water calmer
than a hostage negotiator,
I step out of my kayak
(the way I was taught)
and bum a smoke
from a friendly ling cod.

At the Hamburger Hut in nearby Nakusp,
I order a burger with ketchup
and I'm served a wide-screen TV
depicting the funeral of George W. Bush.
I ask for a side of onion rings.

In the frozen-food section
of Mountain Berry Foods,

a chicken breast looks up at me
and says, "Stuart,
read to me again
from that book about the chicken breast
that saves twenty-six orphans
from a burning bingo hall."

At the corner table of Odin's Pub,
where every table's a corner table,
I am gripped by a tired saviour
with size 17 shoes, a shaggy blue wig,
and a bright red plum for a nose.

In the three-seater outhouse
behind my cabin,
I conduct poetry workshops
for budding spiders.
One of them tries to rhyme
"porridge" with "door hinge."
My publisher dumps me
and signs up the spider.

I thumb a ride with the Valhalla Glacier
but it's going only as far
as the Wal-Mart in Richmond,
where it used to be a greeter.
It stopped in the valley one day,
it tells me,

for a pint at the Silverton Country Inn,
and like so many other
glaciers and mountains,
inlets and lakes,
rabbits and hot springs,
black ants and wasps,
cottonwood and devil's club,
osprey and deer,

it never left.

2 KOOTENAY POEMS

I

one glacier
reaches into the sky
the other
into the lake

when i turn away
they switch places

II

the woodpecker
on my cabin's metal roof
has got a brand new bag

SUBMISSION

I am going to sleep
and I'm praying
that my poem will appear
in *Unhappy Potato Quarterly*.
Lord, let the editorial board
of *Unhappy Potato Quarterly* choose my poem
for inclusion in its delicate, writerly pages.
When I wake up in the morning,
let the editorial board, O Lord,
let the editorial board
of *Unhappy Potato Quarterly* be standing
at the foot of my bed,
looking fondly upon me,
upon my tousled grey hair,
holding my poem in their
delicate, writerly fingers.
Let the Editor Emeritus
of *Unhappy Potato Quarterly*
say to me,
as I lie beneath my threadbare covers,
where only moments ago
I was sleeping
my usual miserable
fitful sleep,
"This poem, Stuart,
this poem accompanied
by a cover letter
threatening suicide if we reject this poem,

is a poem we will publish.
It will waltz alongside the other poems
we will publish, poems we will publish
only to keep your poem company
because we cannot issue an issue of
Unhappy Potato Quarterly
containing only one poem,
even if it is the only poem
deserving of publication."

And I rise from my sheets,
hover above my bed,
equipped now with enough eyes
to meet the eyes of every member
of the *Unhappy Potato Quarterly*
editorial board, including
the intern, including
the intern. And then I realize
that potatoes have eyes, too,
and now I have so many eyes,
and there are all their eyes,
including the eyes of the intern,
and the eyes of the spider dangling from my ceiling,
having just laid a thousand eggs
beneath the flesh of my cheek,
just below my left eye,
and eyes are slimy spherical things
that watch you wherever you go,

and I drift into my closet,
where I cower in a heap of
jackets that no longer fit me.
I hear rustling
in my bedroom,
my mattress being shredded,
the lamp hurled to the floor.
I try to disown my poem
but it clings to me like a leech,
sucks my blood.
I am becoming weak.
O reader, so much
more clever than me,
send for help.

FRAGMENT

Underwater, our behaviour
grows forever, like a
medieval garden dwarf.
But what matters?
We did. We did go away.
In sleep, rain. In dreams,
a chasm. In steam,
a stone. In thinking,
a vast park with no entrance.
We inspect the ordinary,
lament the decrease in services.
Pray for a later time, a remnant of shadow
falling over our blessed eyelids.

SONG

He carried the piano up the stairs.
He carried the piano down the stairs.
He carried the piano up the stairs.
He carried the piano down the stairs.
He sat down and drank a beer.
A bird smacked into his window.
His telephone didn't stop ringing.
The piano was heavy.
He wondered how he would get it up the stairs.

CAPITALISM

I am in a used bookstore.
I am in the poetry section.
I am reaching for a book
that says on its spine
Capitalism, Campbell McGrath.
Behind me are footsteps
creaking up the wooden stairs.
My fingertips grow nearer
to *Capitalism*. The footsteps
grow nearer to the back of me
which has knives sticking out of it.
I am millimetres away
from grasping *Capitalism*
when a hand lands on my shoulder.
The hand is stuck onto an arm
sticking out the right side
of David McFadden.
"Stuart," he says, "I've written some haikus."
And he reaches into his tattered satchel
and pulls out a hardbound notebook.
David McFadden is the author
of many books I love.
These include:
A Knight in Dried Plums
The Poet's Progress
The Art of Darkness
and many others.
When he opens his mouth,

which is located two inches
below his glasses,
haikus come out.
Thus does David McFadden
save me from *Capitalism*
(Campbell McGrath,
Wesleyan University Press,
1990),
and thirty minutes later,
I spill out onto the sidewalk
like an elbowed-over glass of red wine
looking for some pale carpet
to soak into.

THE BOY WHO WAITED THREE MINUTES

Bobby Rottenhead knew that in three minutes everything would be different. Just like his name was different than when his parents had arrived in this country. If they'd kept their original name, he'd now be Bobby Weinberg, but the guy in Immigration had asked Bobby's dad who he was, and Bobby's dad had thought he'd asked *how* he was, and he replied that he had "rottenhead," which in his village back home meant he had a bit of a headache, nothing serious, just a bit of pressure in his temples. So the Immigration guy recorded their names as Irwin and Frieda Rottenhead, and the bureaucracy involved was too daunting to ever change it back.

But in three minutes everything would be different. Bobby Rottenhead was certain of that, though he didn't know what exactly was going to change. Maybe he'd have a third elbow, poking right out the top of his head, or maybe Scotland would turn into an asparagus spear, or maybe the sky and the ocean would switch places. Bobby'd been waiting all his life for these three minutes to pass. Sitting here, in the middle of the football field at Dufferin Heights Junior High School, a cool breeze rustling his curly brown hair, an ant crawling up his left ankle.

He'd been waiting fourteen years for these three minutes to tick by, this seemingly endless one hundred and eighty seconds. In fact, during his bar mitzvah, he'd actually looked at his watch, just to see where the three minutes stood, and that had been a year ago. Soon Bobby would graduate from school, and then he'd go to university, and then he'd be a chartered accountant, or a guy who drew charcoal sketches, and he'd have a wife, or maybe a husband, and a few kids, or maybe none, and soon he'd have to retire, just to make room for younger people, and then he'd be the oldest person on earth to climb a four-metre pyramid of canned niblets at the local SuperFreshMart.

Bobby Rottenhead was pretty excited about that whole niblets thing. But it wasn't going to happen if these three minutes didn't get the hell out of the way. He tapped his foot impatiently and continued to stare at his watch, a watch whose second hand sped recklessly ahead, out of breath, screaming towards a finish line drawn on a gravel road with invisible chalk.

I STEP OFF THE PLANE

after Joe Brainard

I step off the plane. I am buried in heat. It presses against my face.

I step off the plane. I am immediately covered in insects. I cannot feel them, but I can hear them.

I step off the plane. I have seen this country before, perhaps in a film with Edmund O'Brien, directed by a communist with a limp.

I step off the plane. Here the sky pulses. Back home, it just sits there.

I step off the plane. A man in a uniform approaches me, carrying a small purple sack, like the one I kept marbles in as a child. I loosen the yellow cord that seals it, and peer in. A kitten is curled up, its eyes closed: I cannot tell whether it is sleeping or dead. Oh no, sorry — I cannot tell whether *I* am sleeping or dead.

I step off the plane. I've landed in the wrong country.

I step off the plane. I see that I never should have left in the first place. Without going home, I know that everything has changed.

I step off the plane. People here depend on me, but I cannot remember why.

I step off the plane. Now wherever I go, movie music follows me.

ACROSS THE BORDER

"Two people dead, just so we can live without working."
— Bart Tare, in *Gun Crazy*

Mom, there's a disconnect
between the lazy river of the slivered moon
and my whole level of motivation.
It was these things:
the payroll office, the cigarette lighter,
a bundle of crossed-out love poems,
an empty glove clutching a gun.

If you fit all the pieces together,
or go for a stroll arm-in-arm
on the causeway, you will find me
reclining in a fold-out lounge chair,
sipping *jugo de naranja* and
reading whatever I feel like,
and there are a lot of those.

Let me explain, because the newspapers
are written by Gus the plumber. She reached
for the alarm. He went to help her.
My hand spat fire. A foot on the accelerator.
Dark eyes wet beneath dark hair,
a face that said tragedy,
so I kissed it.

Here
in Mexico,
I caress the ears of the deaf.
Children massage my feet.
My life of crime
is a distant memory.

A TRUE HISTORY OF THE NETHERLANDS

Jip and Janneke ride their bikes through the narrow streets.
It is early evening, another perfect day.
A klompje impedes their path.
They fall over and rub their heads, laughing.
"Look at the cute puppy!" says Janneke.
Jip does not see a puppy.
Janneke sees puppies everywhere now.
"Look at the cute puppy!" says Janneke
every two goddamn minutes.
She points and her eyes light up
and she says, "Look at the cute puppy!"
Soon Jip and Janneke draw apart.
They eat their cheese separately.

(The church tower in Gronigen has millions of stairs.
On the beach, women go without tops.
Everybody has a bike!
You can get anywhere in the country
in under ten minutes.
Jews may be hidden behind false walls.
The prostitutes smile and wave through the window.
Patrick lowers his bed from the ceiling,
his apartment is so small.
The windmills perform for adoring tulips.
Everywhere you spit there is water
and the land is as flat as a pancake.
Kim admires the tall ships from her sailboat.
It has never snowed in Maastricht
and also the buildings are 600 years old.)

Several years later in the groentewinkel,
Janneke sees Jip by the hagelslag:
he doesn't know which kind to buy.
There was a time she'd have helped him choose,
a time before the puppies.
Now she carries the world on her shoulders,
a burden she bears without flinching.
If there is a tiny stab in Janneke's heart,
she isn't aware. Everything is about to happen,
you can hear it in the distance,
a comforting rumble that grows by the moment,
a warmth, a canny intelligence,
and that is why the Netherlands
is called the land of love.

IN A VILLAGE JUST OFF EXIT 47

The attic crawlspace was cobwebbed and grim
An earwig peered longingly out the fogged window
On the lawn a dead tulip snapped at the stem
Collapsed after a lesson in cursive Kimbundu

A rabbi drew all of this, using cross-hatch and stipple
While his wife prepared oxygen for her annual climb
A pond erupted suddenly from a negligible ripple
Drenching the synagogue in left-over time

A cloud drifted down from the frame of the sky
Revealing all that was left of the sun, a dark stain
The sleep-deprived jailer hummed a dead lullaby
Cradling a child who flickered like a flame

An unopened letter read, "Blab blab blab blab"
The pockmarked highway declared the afternoon "drab"

BECAUSE ONE THING BUMPED INTO ANOTHER

I was just a young hamburger, a hamburger
wandering from bun to bun, I did not care,
reading Proust and Beckett and Eluard,
dreaming of a tiny apartment in Paris,

while the other burgers played football and
fought in the alleys with switchblades, spilling
condiments in their reckless wake.
At night, I nestled beneath a bed

of sautéed onions and shivered,
an orphan of ground flesh whose
visceral nightmares made sleep a world
of terror. Someone once told me

of a thing called love, and also
a thing called lightning, and I
watched the skies for both,
peered longingly through the frail wisps

of cloud that drifted amidst
the airplanes. I was a young hamburger,
and Paris was just a page in a book
that was wrenched from my grasp

by a dark-suited man with a red necktie
who said that the world had changed.

TV LISTINGS

    Inoffensive
    but confusing fluff
    about a blind plumber
    who unearths a mystery
    that shakes the foundations
    of a small town
    populated entirely
    by hump-backed whales
    with law degrees.
    OK time-waster
    marred by the fact
    that whales are mammals
    when they should be fish.
    Watch for
    cameo appearance
    by Victor Mature
    as the wily
    elbow-pipe salesman.
    Original script
    by Dalton Trumbo
    was trashed by drunk teenagers
    night before filming
    began. Original
    93-minute version
    marks first talking role
    by a rock
    shaped like
    Parker Posey.

MY LAPEL

I

I lose my horoscope.
My horoscope speaks to me.
I, its mother, swim out to sea
and become learning, become decorum.
A flood of monsters
arises at noon and shows us
what it has written.
What it has written
is certainty. Regrets.

II

A breeze diverged from wisdom.
A book grew into the dark corners
of a dank room. To be continued.

III

I mumbled to the frost,
I asked for forgiveness.
I wore a label on my left ankle.
The label said: "The air behaves strangely."
Too late. A voyage of dreams
holds promise. I repeat:

a voyage of dreams holds an air mattress.
I watch the girls' dresses
of smoke, dresses of oak and ivy.
Another time, our opinions were polluted.
I was so ignorant, I cried. I
wrapped myself in wallpaper
and tried to shine like the brightest star.

IV

In darkness, the secrets grew
like huge red flowers, their fumes
an elixir. Success came later and
urgently. It shifted like the steam
of promise. The crows are my children.
The mudslide is my original idea.
I sleep, I pray,
a remnant
with no memory and
no itinerary. A decade
nods, renounces that which is near.
I pin soup on my lapel.
I exist.

ERMINE AND PEARLS

An ermine poked its sleek white head out from a cupboard in the corner of the cabin and looked right at him, as if to say, "Why don't you write a story about an ermine sticking its handsome snout out of a cupboard in the corner of the cabin?" First he had thought maybe it was a rat, then a mink, then an albino weasel, then he remembered it was an ermine, and there was that song about looking good in ermine and pearls. Who sang that song? Was it Pearl Bailey? Or someone white, like the ermine or Ethel Merman? No, it was Marilyn Monroe and maybe Jane Russell and they were coming down this glamorous curving staircase with handsome men in suits on both sides, adoring and escorting them. So he pulled a folding chair up to the little wooden table in the cabin and he started writing. He wrote about giraffes stampeding along a dirt road, late at night, red police lights intermittently illuminating their great straining bodies. And then he heard the crowing of roosters, and he wasn't sure whether they were in his story or outside his cabin.

She said to drag the kayak further up the pebble beach, because the water was rising. He had never dragged the kayak on his own before. He fumbled and shoved and got it right-side up, and there were ropes and handles for dragging. He grasped a loop at one end and tugged, and the kayak began to slide, bumpily, over the pebbles. As he pulled, it became easier. Occasionally he had to scurry to the other end of the boat and push, just to get over a rotting log, but mainly he pulled. The lake crept up the pebbles, following the man pulling the kayak. The sky turned suddenly grey, and rain began to fall. He lugged the kayak as far as the cabin, but the lake followed. The rain soaked through his jean jacket and his denim pants; water pooled in his leather shoes. It was hours before — coughing, sneezing, and gulping for breath — he reached the small town, just a couple of kilometres down the highway. In the middle of the main street, he climbed into the kayak and peered around for the lake.

The moon filtered through the trees that created a canopy over the trail he walked. Every so often the large black dog galloped ahead of him, sniffed, barked, then came running back to trot alongside him. He couldn't remember how long he'd been walking, and whether he was on his way to the logging town, or coming back from it. He recalled seeing a tidy pile of logs gleaming in the dying remnants of the sun, but perhaps that had been yesterday, or the day before. He stopped, and the dog stopped beside him. They both sniffed the air, and the man detected the faintest whiff of smoke. The dog detected mice, deer, coyotes, rotting berries, its own shit from days earlier, and a shoe just a few metres off the trail, where it had lain for thirty years, covered in damp mulch. Before the loggers, there had been miners, and they carried sixty pounds of rocks along this trail, a trail that would soon taper to almost nothing, as it skirted the edge of a precipice that called the man's name.

"I SPEAK ENGLISH, WALL STREET ENGLISH"

In the Métro, at Bastille station,
a bunny rabbit in yellow pyjamas
warns against
trapping our hands
in the doors.
The force of the closing doors
is of a mighty power.
It's all we can do
to clamp our palms
between our knees
to resist
the doors' stubborn pull.

ADJUSTMENT

A building. An office. A boss. A box. Cramped, limbs folded, breath short. I have walked the cracked sidewalks of society; that is to say I have walked. A desk. A phone. A note. Eggs, coffee, aspirin. A boss in a box. A chimp. Clock ticks. A tic. A muffled command. Box rocks. Laughter. I have presided over a cowering, scampering mass; I have dictated. A chimp. A cry. A gasp. An impossible tightness. A list. Numbers. An adjustment. Fists curled. A box. A buzzer. A series of blows. A newspaper. A boss in a box. Hot breath inhaled. A marvellous shutdown of organs. A photo. A family. A window. A shattering. Paper sailing over the city. A grunt. A cry. A chimp. A windowsill. Box teeters. Laughter. Clock ticks. Box tips. A scattering on the sidewalk. I have sailed and I have built; I have destroyed. A cool breeze with a chance of showers. A crack. A boss. A smudge.

50 O'CLOCK

And I went back
to those streets, back
to those streets
made only of footprints.
The sun was a bright yellow
cut-out above. I looked at my watch:
it was 50 o'clock. I was
49 late. But I didn't hurry.
The volcano was rattling,
and the bus, and my skull,
and all around me
children bobbed in plastic buckets,
submerged to their shoulders
in grey soups of water.
It was that hot. Their houses
were made of corrugated metal
and the hoods and doors of cars,
and sides of wooden crates,
and sheets of torn plastic. Everything
was made of something else.
Everything
had fleas. ¡Qué alegre!

BATHURST AND ST. CLAIR, 11:43 PM

I step out of Shoppers' Drug Mart
with a plastic bag in each hand
and it's a warm summer night and I'm
looking into the eyes of David McFadden.
David McFadden is looking into my eyes.
He sits on a milk crate. His hand
is thrust forward, palm up, cupped. Dana
is beside me, she has never met
David McFadden, and now here he is,
it has come to this, Canada's greatest poet
begging change at the entrance to
Shoppers Drug Mart.

                      David stands and we chat,
he's just moved into the neighbourhood, he's
writing, yeah, things are okay, but I'm
really uneasy, and he's not smiling
and I introduce him to Dana and
he smiles. A few moments later we part
and David puts a dollar in the outstretched
palm of the guy on the milk crate
beside his, then walks off towards Raglan.
"I didn't know that was David McFadden,"
Dana tells me. "I just saw this old guy
peering through the windows of Shoppers
Drug Mart and when he saw you,
a big smile came onto his face
and he sat down on that milk crate
and stuck out his hand."

SONNET FOR THE NEW YEAR

We got our heads screwed on just right,
sticking out of our russet turtlenecks,
bobbing like nobody's business.
We got bundles of two-by-fours
lashed to our backs,
and fistfuls of matches

or crazy ideas.
We reach forward with one tentative foot
in this newfangled thing we call "walking"
(the "l" is silent, like our determination,
but also like the first "l" in "llama,"
or the second, I can never remember).

OK, I'm tired now. Let's sit down.
I'm told if we wait, we can do it again.

1 January 2004

LETTER FOR SATURDAY (JANUARY 1, 2005)

Dear pant legs,
I slip my legs
into you. Dear necktie,
I tie you around my neck.
Dear shirt, you hide
my considerable belly,
you warm my freckled arms.
Dear socks, how is
the weather around my feet,
around each separate toe?
Dear door, I slip through
the wood of you
quietly. Dear street,
dusted with snow, you
cradle my car and
pass it along to the grocery store.
Dear unwobbling display
of canned niblets, you nourish me
that I might prepare
for the days ahead,
the days with a new name,
and the people that people them,
the wonderful things they contain.

POEM FOR SUNDAY (JANUARY 1, 2006)

A guy stuck a "New & Improved!" tag
Onto the day. You sauntered to the window
That looked onto the patio
And the moist ravine beyond.
You pulled open the blinds.
One new thing was that
You could actually step through the window,
Through the glass of the window.
Glass is a supercooled liquid
That is hard, brittle, and transparent.
You are the opposite. I like your smile.
I like how you write in the margins of books.
The patio stones like how you pad across them
In your bare feet in winter.
The moist ravine likes your attitude,
Your commitment to separating
Compost from trash. The rest
Of the world, the things
In the world, are taken by you too.
I pull on my socks,
And, Homer-like,
Write this poem.

RAZOVSKY AND THE RIVER OF BLINDNESS

Razovsky waded through the water, through reeds and bobbing plastic burger containers. Scum swam around his thighs, regrouping behind him, laughing. O scum! Televisions splashed in the rocks near the shore; a man waving a megaphone filled all the screens. Above him, a sun of yellow construction paper fluttered behind some clouds, coughed like a grandfather, fell asleep on the couch. An invisible marching band followed along at the banks, playing the anthem of each shtetl he passed. Razovsky had these eyebrows that crashed against his eyes. He cracked his knuckles and lapped at his lips. Razovsky pushed against the wind, as loose book pages flapped past his face: Polish, Yiddish, Russian, Hebrew, English, German. He'd been walking this river since before he was born and today he'd step out and see his own feet and feel the ground beneath them, sometimes solid, sometimes giving, and he'd walk up to a shack and pass through a door and sit down to eat dinner and he'd look at each face at the table, and each would have a nose in the middle, and he too would have a nose: everyone would have a nose and each nose two nostrils — so many nostrils! — and he would begin to tell everyone about his years in the river, and the glorious shimmer of the moon would pour from his mouth.

1 January 2007

NOTES

This book is for Dana Samuel, my favourite artist.

Thanks to Kristi-Ly Green for sparking "Robots at Night," and to Ron Padgett, in whose workshop I wrote "In a Village Just Off Exit 47" and who offered input on another poem. Kevin Connolly and Dana Samuel provided valuable feedback on many of these pieces as well.

I wrote the italicized poems while listening to John Ashbery's poems "Flow Chart," "Girls on the Run," and "Self-Portrait in a Convex Mirror" read aloud during various of my workshops. I wrote several other of these poems in my Poetry Boot Camps: I thank the participants of those sessions for their stamina, creativity, and camaraderie.

Some of these poems appeared, sometimes in earlier versions, in the magazines *dig.*, *Filling Station*, *Peter F. Yacht Club*, *Taddle Creek*, and *Walrus*; as leaflets from Proper Tales Press; in the chapbook *Robots at Night* (Proper Tales); and in the anthologies *Time to Kill Boss* (Proper Tales) and *Surreal Estate: 13 Canadian Poets Under the Influence* (The Mercury Press). Thanks to appropriate editors.

I'm grateful to Brian Kaufman of Anvil Press for taking on this project, and to Gary Clement for creating the cover.

Thanks, finally, to the bookstores that have stocked my books, the schoolteachers and reading organizers who've hosted me, and those who've bought my books, come to my readings, and told me what they thought.

ABOUT THE AUTHOR

Stuart Ross is a Toronto fiction writer, poet, editor, and creative-writing instructor. He has been active in the Toronto small-press scene since the mid-1970s. Stuart is the author of four previous spiney poetry collections, including the widely acclaimed *Hey, Crumbling Balcony! Poems New & Selected* (ECW Press). His collection *Farmer Gloomy's New Hybrid* (ECW Press) was one of seven books short-listed for the 2000 Trillium Book Award, given to the best book of any genre published in Ontario. Stuart is also the author of the fiction collection *Henry Kafka and Other Stories* (The Mercury Press), as well as three novellas and the book of personal essays *Confessions of a Small Press Racketeer* (Anvil Press). He is also editor of the seminal anthology *Surreal Estate: 13 Canadian Poets Under the Influence* (The Mercury Press) and has edited several literary magazines, most recently the poetry journal *Syd & Shirley*. He is currently the Fiction & Poetry Editor for *This Magazine*. Stuart's work has appeared in scores of journals in Canada and the U.S., including *Harper's, Walrus, Geist, Rampike, The Capilano Review, Taddle Creek,* and *Bomb Threat Checklist*, as well as in several anthologies and textbooks. His column "Hunkamooga" appears in *sub-Terrain*. *I Cut My Finger* is Stuart's first full-length poetry book in four years. Visit his online home at www.hunkamooga.com.